PARNELL: A MEMOIR

Essays and Texts in Cultural History V

PARNELL: A MEMOIR
Edward Byrne

EDITED BY FRANK CALLANAN

THE LILLIPUT PRESS
1991

First published in 1991 by
THE LILLIPUT PRESS LTD
4 Rosemount Terrace, Arbour Hill,
Dublin 7, Ireland.

A CIP record for this
title is available from
The British Library.

ISBN 0 946640 82 3

Cover photograph by William Lawrence

Series editor: W.J. Mc Cormack

Cover design by Jarlath Hayes
Set and formatted in 10 on 12.5 Palatino
on an Apple Macintosh II si (*Quark Xpress*)
and printed in Dublin by
Colour Books Ltd of Baldoyle

CONTENTS

ILLUSTRATIONS

EDITOR'S PREFACE

This series, called ETCH, Essays and Texts in Cultural History, fills the gap between short articles in obscure journals and lengthy books at inflated prices. The field is Irish cultural history in the broadest sense, including works in both Gaelic and English, non-literary material, and foreign commentary on Irish culture. The series includes essays originally commissioned, reprints of valuable items from the past, translations . . . indeed any kind of material which can increase awareness of cultural history within Ireland, cultural history as it affects Ireland.

Had Parnell not existed it would have been necessary to invent him. How else could the cult of Anglo-Irish literature have established itself, god-less? James Joyce's early indoctrination in the religion of the fallen Parnell is well known, and the power of the dinner-table scene in *A Portrait of the Artist as a Young Man* is demonstrated in those re-enactments of the occasion which take place each year on location in the house in Bray, County Wicklow. Yeats too declared himself a Parnellite, though one should note carefully how very late these declarations were made. All the poems invoking Parnell were written in the 1930s, when the 'strong man' notion of politics was exercising its pernicious effect on the poet.

Other, less titanic, figures of Anglo-Irish literature have also investigated the legend of the Chief, notably Seán Ó Faoláin in his longer fiction. In 1958 Herbert Howarth gave to his study of *The Irish Writers 1880-1940* the subtitle, 'Literature under Parnell's star'. More recently, James Plunkett's employment of James Larkin in *Strumpet City* is really an adaptation of the literary myth of Parnell to a different social context, that of the Dublin working class. Now it is rumoured that Sherlock Holmes is to be proved the assassin of Parnell in a short story rescued from the posthumous papers of John H. Watson MD.

The central feature of the present memoir also has its literary character, albeit a less sublime one. Parnell's relations with the newspapers of his day form a valuable link between him and the world of writing. Parnell himself appears to have avoided the act of writing to the greatest practical extent. There are no Parnell philosophies, correspondences, prison memoirs or prophetic legacies. All that kind of thing was left by him – and by conservative Irish leaders after him – to the radicals. If you want to *read* the Irish Party you must turn to Davitt. Parnell, by contrast, adapted the spoken word to the age of mass journalism with something akin to the genius of a dictaphone in revolt against the office manager. The tactic of obstruction in the House of Commons by means of 'filibustering' demonstrated the endless recyclability of spoken language into, and then out of, written reports: the Aeolus episode in Joyce's *Ulysses* is comparable, with Bloom fearful of what might happen should the overseer of the newspaper get paralysed on the job. 'Monkeydoodle the whole thing,' is Bloom's guess, and the phrase might be used as a casual summary of Parnell's intention with regard to parliamentary procedure.

Historians concede that the events and personalities upon which their predecessors concentrated are essentially mediated through texts. The 'deeds and doers' version of history is replaced by a stricter attention to the textuality of all evidence. This is not the same proposition as the ludicrous one declaring all histories fictions. Parnell is peculiarly a sensitive case, because of his own avoidance of writing, because of his contrived volubility, and because of the coincidence of his rise and fall with genuine extensions of newspaper power. Yet literary 'placings' can still be revealing, if interpreted as a form of metaphor. Parnell operated somewhere between King Lear and Citizen Kane. All memoirs of him should be valued, and suspected.

W J M

INTRODUCTION

Edward Byrne, the author of this memoir, is a largely forgotten collaborator, adviser and friend of Charles Stewart Parnell: a self-effacing figure behind a forbiddingly terse leader. Born in Tuam, County Galway, in 1847, Byrne was educated in St Jarlath's College. He worked as a journalist on the *Tuam Herald* and then on the *Tuam News*. At the age of twenty-five he became the editor of the Belfast *Morning News*. Recruited to the *Freeman's Journal* by its proprietor, Edmund Dwyer Gray, he started in the literary department to become the paper's editor during the halcyon days of Parnellism. The *Freeman's Journal* played a critical role in consolidating Parnell's leadership and authority, as if in atonement for the hostility displayed at the outset of his career. By the late 1880s it had become the authoritative journalistic voice of Parnellism.[1]

Byrne's allegiance was more ardent than that of his employer. The *Tuam News* obituary of Byrne cast him as an unsung Parnellite hero:

Always a thorough Nationalist . . . Mr Byrne devoted his life in his quiet retiring manner to the advocacy of Home Rule. During that glorious epoch in the latter history of this country, when the Irish Party became the admiration of the civilized world and many public men were making glorious reputations in the arena of Irish politics, there was one man who, silently, unobtrusively, without ostentation or display, did a hero's work.

The *Freeman's Journal* sustained Parnell through the ordeal of the Pigott forgeries and the proceedings of the Special Commission which followed. When Captain W.H. O'Shea instituted divorce proceedings in which Parnell was named as co-respondent on 24 December 1889, the paper panegyrically invoked the false precedent of his triumph before the Special

Commission: 'He rose calmly' above the means resorted to against him, 'and trampled them underfoot, as an Archangel might stamp upon a many-headed dragon.'[2] The bombastic extravagance belied Parnell's vulnerability.

In the wake of the shock of the divorce decree and Gladstone's declaration against Parnell, Byrne struggled to shore up the crumbling edifice of Parnell's power. The paper ringingly endorsed the Irish leader, and in the critical early stage of the crisis did everything possible to further Parnell's strategy of exaggerating the level of popular support on which he could count in Ireland, as he sought to unnerve and overwhelm the majority of the Irish Party at Westminster opposed to him.

It was in the *Freeman's Journal* that Parnell, on 29 November 1890, published his high-rolling manifesto 'to the people of Ireland', an account of his interview with Gladstone at Hawarden which put in issue the Liberal leader's intentions in relation to critical aspects of the Home Rule Bill to be introduced on his return to power.

Both Byrne and the *Freeman's Journal's* London correspondent, James M. Tuohy, collaborated closely with Parnell through the six days of debates in Committee Room 15, covered by the paper in an acknowledged triumph of contemporary reporting.[3]

Byrne's belief in the necessity of sustaining Parnell never wavered. 'By voice and pen he preached the policy right strenuously and well.' (*Irish Daily Independent*) 'He saw his course, and he walked along manfully and proudly by the side of Parnell. His pen did wonderful service in those days of bitter struggle. His personality was a power.' (*Evening Herald*)

Byrne was, however, unswayed by the premature triumphalism of the Parnellite camp in Dublin, and alive to Parnell's political vulnerability. He realized the dangers of an all-out conflict for the maintenance of Parnell's enduring influence in Irish politics. In the tense hiatus between the schism of the Irish Party in Committee Room 15 and the North Kilkenny election, Byrne acted as an emissary for the Archbishop of Dublin in a curious peace initiative, which would have established the archbishop as the politico-moral arbitrator of the split. Unsurprisingly, the mission aborted.[4]

2

The direction of the *Freeman's Journal* grew increasingly apprehensive and anxious to procure a settlement. Immediately after the split in Committee Room 15, the paper urged that Dillon and O'Brien be invited back from America to France, to confer with the contending factions. Edward Byrne spent Christmas and the New Year in Boulogne, where Parnell joined O'Brien on 30 December in an endeavour to ensure the successful outcome of the negotiations, which again proved futile.[5]

The *Freeman's Journal* came under clerical and conservative nationalist attack. With the launching of the *National Press* by T.M. Healy on 7 March 1891, the paper's unchallenged status of leading nationalist metropolitan daily was forfeit. The chauvinistic populism of Healy's oratory and leader-writing inaugurated a revolution in Irish politics and journalism. The *Freeman's* shrill and *démodé* rhetoric of fidelity to Parnell was no match for the ferocious demotic vigour of its rival. As circulation waned, so did the allegiance of Edmund Dwyer Gray *fils*, who had taken over from his late father. The volte-face of the *Freeman's Journal* proved tortuously protracted: Gray awaited the release of John Dillon and William O'Brien from Galway jail, and then struggled to impose his will upon a recalcitrantly Parnellite board of directors.

At the first shareholders' meetings convened to determine the policy of the paper, Byrne seconded T.C. Harrington's resolution of confidence in the existing directors. He pointed out that no member of the board or the editorial committee had dissented from the decision to support Parnell. The paper had stated from the outset

that their business with Parnell was political, and that the business of Ireland with him was political . . . I say we have no right to discuss the moral question. If the press of the country set up a right to hold an inquisition into a man's private life, where will it end?

Byrne's speech was a classic statement of the principles of Parnellism:

If Mr Parnell were dead or were removed from political life by any cause we would stand out for the same policy . . . The curse of Ireland has been this weak-kneed yielding to every suggestion and hint from English parties (hear, hear) . . . We are threatened today with a recrudescence of Whiggery in Ireland, with the sending back of the country to the old slavish days before Mr Parnell and the League taught every man in Ireland to stand erect, and to regard every other man as his equal (hear, hear).[6]

At the second, and decisive, meeting, Byrne dissociated himself with dignity from his former assistant, the barrister E.H. Ennis, once a vehement Parnellite, who had reneged to support Gray's proposed change of policy. Byrne deprecated Ennis's contention that journalists, like barristers, as Byrne put it, should have no convictions on the subjects they wrote about:

He did not wish to attach any importance to his personality, but he was not a 'bread and butter' journalist. Rather than write against his convictions he would retire from journalism altogether and would have to starve if things went so far as that.[7]

Many of the *Freeman*'s staff were made of sterner stuff than the shareholders, and did not hesitate to make what Parnell called 'this cruel severance'. His comment that 'it is no light thing for a journalist to part company with a great newspaper in which he has taken a pride, whose growth he has watched and shared for so many years, and whose progress has been a joy to him', showed his sensitivity to the rending of Byrne and others from the paper on which they had long worked.[8]

The paper declared against Parnell on 24 September 1891, less than two weeks before his death. Parnell's last energies were expended on the establishment of a national newspaper, the *Irish Daily Independent*, which first appeared, after his death, on 18 December 1891. Anticipating the *Freeman*'s defection, he declared: 'The profession of journalism is a great and powerful one in these days. It is likely to become more influential as the years go by . . . the press is becoming ever mightier than the politician.' The task of establishing a new paper needed to be faced as 'in these days politics and journalism run very much together, and the trend is more and more to combine the two'.[9]

Byrne became the editor of the *Irish Daily Independent*, a position he held until poor health forced him to resign.[10] He did not live to witness the final ignominy of its takeover from 1 September 1900 by the diehard anti-Parnellite entrepreneur, William Martin Murphy.

Personally as well as politically, the split was a catastrophe for Byrne. As the *Tuam News* remarked, his continued support of Parnell entailed 'great personal sacrifices which to a man of his temperament were indeed bitter'. His colleague Michael McDonagh describes him, after the defection of the *Freeman's Journal*, going out 'to struggle with poverty until he died not long afterwards'.[11] According to T.M. Healy, Byrne,'a jaunty Galway man', died 'almost shoeless and shirtless'.[12]

He was a distinguished journalist, and a fine leader-writer. Familiarly known as the 'doctor', he did much to encourage his younger colleagues. The *Tuam News* commented that he was 'never known to have any man dismissed in any of the offices with which he was connected'. He was elected a fellow of the prestigious Institute of Journalists which he helped to found. There was, wrote *The Irish Times*, 'no more intellectual member of his profession'. He died on 13 October 1899 in Tuam, at the age of fifty-two.

II

Edward Byrne's evocation of Parnell appeared in the *Irish Weekly Independent* of 8 October 1898, a year before his own death. It is a political record of some importance, and a haunting text of the Parnell myth.

It was at Maryborough, in the autumn of 1881, that Byrne heard Parnell address a public meeting for the first time. Their close collaboration relates to the later period, after Gladstone's espousal of Home Rule in 1886.

Byrne was not privy to Parnell's dealings with the ruling Conservatives in 1885, although he does make the plausible assertion that Sir Henry Drummond Wolff was involved in the negotiations between the Irish and the Tories which eventuated in the defeat of the Gladstone government on 9 June 1885. Byrne's stumbling on the fact that the Dwyer Grays had dined with Lord Carnarvon, the Conservative Lord Lieutenant, and his wife at the Viceregal Lodge serves to highlight the difficulties of conducting *haute politique* in the intimate, gossiping stasis of the Irish capital. He asserts that it was at this meeting, the occurrence of which was not previously known, that the

5

arrangements were made for Parnell's meeting with Carnarvon in London.

Byrne called to see the Irish leader at his hunting lodge in Aughavanagh, close to Avondale, in August 1888. It was immediately prior to the opening of the hearings of the Special Commission, charged with inquiring into the *Times* allegations against Parnell and his collaborators of complicity in the Phoenix Park murders, centred on the Pigott forgeries. The business, a press release on Parnell's part, was swiftly transacted: Byrne gives an idea of how clear, precise and economic were Parnell's political arrangements and provides a rare evocation of a relaxed Parnell at home in Wicklow, with a memorable still life of the lunch table's 'most rustic *mélange*, ham and grouse and domestic fowl and fruit and tea and wine and whiskey, taken from the window embrasures and queer recesses, with all sorts and conditions of china and plate and glass'.

Byrne's assertion that Parnell did not intend to become the Prime Minister of a Home Rule administration, but rather Home Secretary, or perhaps even Prime Minister, at Westminster, is to be dated to the political zenith following the discrediting and suicide of Pigott. For Parnell, taking office at Westminster after the enactment of Home Rule had two obvious reasons: it would have enabled him to insulate himself from the disillusionment which would beset a nationalist government in Ireland as grossly exaggerated popular expectations were disappointed; it would also have permitted him to protect and entrench a Home Rule *régime* by the tight marshalling of nationalist power at Westminster. Yet it is more unlikely that Parnell did not decide against a strategy which risked appearing to derogate from the logic of legislative independence. The intention imputed by Byrne is moreover difficult to reconcile with Parnell's public declarations on the role of Irish nationalist parliamentarians in Westminster after Home Rule.

Byrne's observation, as restrictively construed, suggests the radical exhaustiveness of Parnell's strategic thinking, and recalls the seemingly excellent prospects of the Liberal-

PARNELL'S PARLIAMENTARY PUPPETS.   THE STRINGS IN A TANGLE

Nationalist alliance, and Parnell's stature within it, which, in the glad confident morning prior to the divorce crisis, stood higher than any of Gladstone's lieutenants and putative successors.

Byrne accompanied Parnell to his meetings at Nottingham and Liverpool around the time of his triumphal visit to Gladstone at Hawarden on 18-19 December 1889, which was to be the subject of bitter controversy in the split. Byrne's account conveys Parnell's sanguine and expansive temper as the flowing tide of the Liberal-Nationalist alliance swept faster onwards giving no intimation of the dissatisfaction Parnell would express in his manifesto of the following year.

Byrne evokes Parnell's intransigent and combative spirit, as he desperately tried to retain the allegiance of his friends and supporters, by appealing to old loyalties and – a favourite device – seeking Liberal assurances in relation to the provisions of the Home Rule legislation to be enacted. He tormentedly rehearses the controversy of the manifesto, struggling to reconcile its allegations with Parnell's state of mind and public statements at the time of the Hawarden visit.

His somewhat strained treatment of the issue reveals the suppressed unease with which even Parnell's most loyal collaborators followed him into the wilderness of the split. Byrne needed to believe; he was desperately eager to accept the allegations of the manifesto, but unable to do so. He tried to persuade himself that Parnell was at least sincere, hence his citing of the leader's private comments at the time of the debates in Committee Room 15 as if they somehow provided corroboration.

Byrne perfectly exemplifies the crisis of Parnellite allegiance in the split. The inner political circle of Parnellism was comprised largely of those who were actuated by considerations of affection, loyalty and gratitude, fortified by deep anger at the manner in which Parnell had been treated by the majority of the party, and by the Catholic Church in Ireland, after Gladstone's intervention. Yet they baulked at their leader's harsh and remorseless political logic, epitomized in what they regarded as the realpolitik-run-berserk of the manifesto. Parnell, however, insisted on treating the split as a contest of raw political capacity in the independent opposition. While badly worsted up to the time of his death, he repeatedly instanced an almost terrifying political acumen, which outclassed any of his nationalist contemporaries.

The blank incomprehension which Parnell's fierce resolve in the split elicited among those sympathetic to him was articulated by Byrne's former colleague, James Tuohy, who wrote of

the impassive resolution with which he argued down all suggestions, from whatever source they proceeded, which had for their object the real conservation of his influence and position by bringing about his temporary retirement. Strange and striking a man as Mr Parnell was in every respect, he never presented so unsolvable a psychological problem to his friends as during the last few months.[13]

Byrne's memoir is historically important. But most of all it is a personal testament, a moving remembrance of Parnell, notable for its portrayal of the Irish leader in tranquil, almost playful, mood, and for its evocation of his dry wit. It is also a rare account of what may be called Parnell's table talk. To Byrne Parnell lifted the severe mask of reticence (clamping down the vizier only in response to Byrne's unguarded enquiry as to the vanity of public men). Byrne conveys Parnell's private charm and clarity of mind, and something of how he won and held the allegiance of those who knew him.

Byrne observed Parnell closely, and his reminiscences of the Irish leader rebut the snide but intriguing comment of the rancidly anti-Parnellite Sergeant A.M. Sullivan:

Of all those associated with him, I wonder how many really knew Parnell . . . It is amusing to note how many have published their impressions of intimacy with Parnell. Those who really knew him spoke of him but little, and of him wrote nothing.[14]

PARNELL: A MEMOIR

It was a real Irish day with the tear and the smile in its eye when I first saw Charles Stewart Parnell at a public meeting. I had met him in a great newspaper office in which I was leader-writer at the time, and in which I was afterwards editor for several years; but his quietude – an almost imposing quietude – of manner gave me a curiosity and a desire to see for myself, and not through the medium of reporters, how a new personality was fascinating the people, my countrymen and country-women. So, in some month of the autumn of 1881, I took occasion to go down to Maryborough, where Mr Parnell was announced to speak. I think it was a Land League Convention. I know it was an organized assemblage; and I shall never forget the figure in the wagonette stiffly bowing to the enthusiastic throng. It was tall, slender, and ill-dressed. Mr Parnell comman-ded attention at that time by the pallor of his face, and the curious shimmering brilliancy of his eyes. They were a yel-lowish brown in the pupil, and darkened and became intense and almost black, as he grew coldly earnest. The usual speeches were made. As well as I can recall, the late Mr Lalor MP and a Canon O'Keeffe were the principal local speakers, but the lion of the day was Mr Parnell. I shall never forget the close of the brief address which he delivered. It was so naively frank. He said it was his determination and that of the organization which he presided over that all the working-classes of the country, working either by hand or brain, should have a fair subsistence in the country, and he ended: 'If there be anything after that left for the landlords they may have it!'[1] It was grim – wasn't it?

Without referring to notes or diary, my impression is that a few days after the demonstration to which I have alluded Mr Parnell was arrested.

I saw Mr Parnell more than once on business in Kilmainham Jail. He was lodged in the infirmary, and looked very delicate indeed. The situation was an extraordinary one. The statesman, since dead, who had caused a general jail delivery in King Bomba's Two Sicilies was now himself the jailer of several Irish members of the Parliament of which he was the leader. Mr Parnell was drily caustic on Mr Gladstone. But he chafed under his confinement and the restraint to which he was subjected and one could easily perceive that he longed to be out and in the fray. It was at this period the 'No Rent' Manifesto was issued, and I shall never forget the expression – half puzzled, half amused – that passed over Mr Parnell's face when he read Archbishop Croke's denunciation of it, which I brought up to him.

These were desultory memories and reminiscences; so we shall jump, you and I, or public, to the year Mr Parnell went to Hawarden. I was with him, as I had been in nearly all the crucial epochs of a political life studded with crises. We had been together at Nottingham, where the Institute of Journalists met this year, and where he got the reception of a king. It was more than a princely reception. Mounted police surrounded the carriage as he drove through the streets from the railway station. Their presence was necessary in order to keep the pressure of the concourse off the centre of attraction. He spoke at night in a very large hall to a house packed from floor to ceiling. It was the best speech I ever heard him make. His eloquence astonished me, for he was not a fluent man. His talent lay rather in terseness and crispness. But at Nottingham he literally let himself out, and, like ice breaking up under the rays of a warm sun, he swept the people off their feet by an unexpected volume of eloquence and oratory. I sat behind him, proud and surprised and delighted. He had captured the English people, and, bursting the barriers of his habitual reserve, he became for the nonce an ardent and impassioned orator. It is curious how the nature of a man breaks out. There is a phrase the father of which is Parnell, 'I will take off my coat to it', and that night, in Nottingham, he wore, entering the public hall, a light overcoat above dress clothes. I shall never forget the vigour with which, divesting himself at the moment of his overcoat, he advanced to the front of the platform, amidst a salvo of salutes which no hundred and one guns announcing the occasion of a sovereign could attempt to mimic, imitate or rival. It was a gesture preluding the best speech of his brilliant career.[2] Next morning we were to leave for Hawarden. The crush in the streets and at the station was almost a replica at his departure of his arrival. He had arranged that I should occupy the same carriage with him, and he held open the door from the inside while I forced my way through the crowd with difficulty. I had procured all the newspapers, and he had some himself; but I had hardly lifted myself into the carriage when a gentlemanly-looking man stepped quickly in after me, and put out his hand to Mr Parnell, greeting him heartily. Mr Parnell looked sharply and inquisitively at me, and I returned the gaze. The train moved out of the station, and the strange gentleman commenced to describe the country through which we were passing. It was delightful weather, and everything was looking at its best. Our companion evidently knew every inch of the road. He pointed out even the scene of a famous battle in English history. He never drew bridle; he never ceased talking. Mr Parnell's and my own scanning of the newspapers, to read their reports and comments on the previous night's meeting and the antecedent reception, was of the most perfunctory character. Our lively companion monopolized both time and attention. At last we came to Crewe, and Mr Parnell, nodding towards me to follow, stepped out of the carriage into a curious and cheering crowd, awaiting the train to get a glimpse of the man of the time. Our companion quickly followed Mr Parnell, and immediately became the centre of a group of intensely interested and vivacious men and women, all of whom he appeared to know personally. I was just descending from the carriage when Mr Parnell, returning, beckoned me not to stir. I backed into my seat, and Parnell smilingly said, as he reseated himself, 'I thought you knew him.' 'I thought,' I answered, 'he was a friend of yours because he shook hands with you.' 'Oh!' said Mr Parnell, 'of course I saw in a moment that he was a stranger, but it was too late to change carriages, which I wished to do here, in order that we might have privacy for our interview. Do you know who he is? He is a commercial traveller for Colman's mustard in the midland counties.'[3] And as the train steamed out of Crewe, we still saw our friend of the morning narrating to all his acquaintances his experience of a journey with Mr Parnell, and he evidently was the hero of the hour!

I accompanied Mr Parnell to Hawarden, where he dined and slept, and he was for four hours closeted with Mr Gladstone. I had returned to Chester. Mr Parnell engaged to dine with me at the Queen's Hotel next day at four o'clock. I had dinner prepared for him, as time was limited, we both having to go on to Liverpool that evening. He seemed to be in the best health and spirits. He drank, I remember, a flask of still hock. When we were finishing dinner, which was of a very simple kind, I took the opportunity of saying, 'Mr Parnell, as a journalist I am obliged to ask you what occurred between the Grand Old Man and you?' He turned that most pleasant look on me, and with twinkling eyes, said, 'Well, I know you do not expect me to tell you, but I will say this, the old gentleman did most of the talking!' That was the famous conversation of which Mr Parnell, after the split, gave a version, which Mr Gladstone categorically denied; but it was in that interview the terms of the Home Rule Bill which followed were arranged.

We left Chester together, for Liverpool, where Mr Parnell had a superb reception at the Reform Club, and where I was charmed to meet, foremost in the ranks of those greeting him, four Irishmen, townsmen of my own – two brothers, local medical doctors, Drs John and Alexander Bligh, a solicitor and town councillor, named Lynskey, and a naval medical doctor, John Conway, who, I think, was then attached to the training ship. The banquet was a splendid affair. The chairman was the president of the National Liberal Union, Mr Ellis, and the speeches were laudatory, long, and liberal.

Mr Parnell's reply to the toast of his health as the 'Guest of the Evening' was the longest and, I may add, the most laboured, in my humble opinion, I had ever heard him deliver. I cannot at this distance of time recall the exact length of it; but my recollection is that it extended over an hour and a half. It was in marked contrast with his speech of two nights before at Nottingham on his way to Hawarden, which was sharp-spirited,

The Whitehall Review, February 10th, 1881.

The Parliamentary Coup d'État. — February 3rd, 1881.

At the Bar (Expulsion of Mr Parnell)
Mr Chamberlain
Mr Wright   The Speaker
Lord Hartington
Mr Childers   Capt Gosset   Mr Kirkby
Mr Forster   Mr Parnell

Sir W Dyce   Mr Parl. Smith
Mr Rufford Northcote
Mr Obranne   Mr Sullivan
Mr O'Donnell

In the Lobby—After the Expulsion
Mr O'Kelly   Mr Arthur Moore   Mr Biggar-Tray
Mr Healy   Mr Parnell   Mr Tuker
Mr T. M. Sullivan   Mr Healy
Mr T. P. Sullivan   Mr Callan   Mr Dillon

15

THE IRISH FRANKENSTEIN.

"THE BANEFUL AND BLOOD-STAINED MONSTER . . . YET WAS IT NOT MY MASTER TO THE VERY EXTENT THAT IT WAS MY CREATURE? . . . HAD I NOT BREATHED INTO IT MY OWN SPIRIT?" . . . (*Extract from the Works of* C. S. PARNELL, M.P.)

16

and sufficiently short. He seemed in the Liverpool Reform Club to qualify everything, to be weighed with pledges which he only half relished, and to have sundry misgivings. It was as if his sensitive mind had a premonition of Punic Faith and perfidious Albion, and that it trembled like a delicate instrument responsive to the forces swaying it. But the banquet was a huge success. He went out to sup and sleep at the suburban residence of the chairman, a delightful old abbey place, and there in the morning was visited by Mr Andrew Kettle, and lectured on the Land Question, and by the writer of these miscellaneous memories.[4]

I remember when the *Times* Commission, otherwise the impeachment of Parnell, was pending, I interviewed him at Aughavanaugh during the grouse season. My wife and I went down the previous evening and slept in the hotel at the foot of the mountain, whence we dropped up to the barracks built to put down the outlaw, Michael Dwyer, and then occupied by the man regarded in millions of English hearts as not less an outlaw who was to be crushed by fair means or foul, by Pigott's forgery or open force. When the car upon which we drove reached the old swing-gate opening on the barracks, we were met by a sort of gamekeeper, tall, suspicious-visaged, and deterrent, with a shaggy, savage-looking dog at his heels of the half-breed cur kind so frequent in Irish villages and so snappish and vicious. I saluted the man; he scowled; the dog growled. Two omens! I asked the human custodian of the place 'Is Mr Parnell at home?' He growled out bluntly, not less ominously than had his attendant spirit, that he was not. I ventured to remark that that was strange, as I had an appointment with him. A change of expression came over the janitor's face, but still it was distrustful. The dog also brightened up; his sour muzzle somewhat softened its surliness, and there actually seemed an indication that that appendage which is euphemized as the hairy index of the canine mind, would wag. At this moment my then youngish eyes discerned a figure descending the mountain mounted on a heavy-looking horse, with game-bags straddled across the animal's shoulders. 'That's Mr Parnell,' said I, 'coming down there after a shoot.' 'Oh! you know him, then,' said the keeper, 'are you —?' 'I am', replied I, jumping off the car – for the original expressions on my receivers' faces had relaxed – and running through the gate towards Mr Parnell, who was very pleased to see me, and showed it in his best form. The first thing he said, after the usual greetings, was – 'I suppose you think these bags are filled with grouse. They are not. I hardly ever shoot now. I don't care for it.[5] The others are up the mountain. I have been picking ore. These are specimens. They contain gold [handing me one out of the contents of the bag], as you may see.'

The stone did sparkle like

'. . . our Lagenian mine.'

The tiny glittering specks

'. . . all over the surface shine!'

We, three, the lady, he, and I, entered the barracks or lodge, and, ascending the rugged stairs, came to a large roomy apartment in the middle of which was an oval table strewn all over, or, rather, littered with papers or letters in a by no means sweet disorder. We chatted pleasantly on various topics for some time, Mr Parnell became most unusually voluble. His simplicity of character gleamed out, for instance, when a question arose. I am under the middle height. Either my wife, who is tall, or I asked him what height he was. I am six feet, he answered, with a faint radiancy of innocent pride in his eye, and, suiting the action to the word, he stood up and, asking the lady to rise, they put back to back, and, knowing her height, I measured the difference and found Mr Parnell a little over six feet. He would be six feet in his stockings. After lunch, which was a most rustic *mélange*, ham and grouse and domestic fowl and fruit and tea and wine and whiskey, taken from the window embrasures and queer recesses with all sorts and conditions of china and plate and glass, we, he and I, began to talk business. At this time everything looked as black and gloomy as they well could. Imagine my surprise when, beginning an interview, which was to appear in the then leading newspaper of Ireland, of which I was editor, the next morning, the patriot, practically impeached for murder and high treason, said, 'Write we will open thus: "Before a week of the Commission has expired, Mr McDonald,

18

the manager of *The Times* will be in the dock."'

I looked at him. 'Mr Parnell,' I interrupted, 'that is too strong; the public won't stomach it; they will think we are bluffing them.'

'It is true, though,' he retorted, 'begin as I say.' The interview proceeded. It appeared in the newspaper already alluded to, the next morning,[6] my wife and I having returned to Dublin that night. But I excised the opening sentence, which he had stuck to. I judged it too strong for general consumption at the juncture. I preferred and deemed it better, in the temper of the time, to let matters develop themselves. But Mr Parnell, *mens conscia recti*, was confident and bold.

Long after, when he was the master of the very masses that had thirsted for his blood, he and I were together – indeed it was, if I recall aright, on our way to Hawarden – he suddenly turned towards me and said – 'Why did you not publish the opening sentence at that interview which I gave you at Aughavanaugh before the *Times* Commission?' He repeated it word for word. It was one of his singular characteristics that he remembered, liberatim or verbatim, what he said on the many occasions when I interviewed him, as if he had arranged and shelved in his lucid brain the whole statement ready for use and after reference, his words being carefully selected with no redundancy, with directness straight as a die.[7]

I said in extenuation, so to speak, what I had urged on the eve of the appearance of the very remarkable and even momentous interview. He mildly retorted, 'You see, I was right.' 'Well,' I acknowledged, 'if you were not exactly right, you were very near it; if Mr McDonald, the manager of *The Times*, who bought the forged letter from Pigott, was not in the dock, he deserved to be.'

They are all dead now; and Parnell might be called the most popular man in Parliament at the close of the Commission, which opened upon him before a hostile country, jaundiced with saffrony suspicion, and on the pounce to strike with the malevolence of long pent-up malice.

I was with Mr Parnell all during the split and the virtual disruption of the Irish Party. He habitually stayed at the

Westminster Palace Hotel in London during that period. I customarily used to go to see him there from Morley's in Trafalgar Square, which was the hotel I resorted to, and resided in. His habit was, after some of those stormy meetings towards the close of the year of the split, to retire to the smoking-room of the Westminster Palace Hotel, and there discuss the situation with his friends, very few, but amongst whom I had the privilege of being numbered. He unquestionably conveyed all through that period of trouble the idea that he had a way out of the difficulty of the Divorce Court; at the same time that he evidently held in the most complete contempt what was called 'the Nonconformist Conscience', and sovereignly distrusted Mr Gladstone and the other Liberal leaders. He, over and over again, stated in those interviews of mine with him that Sir William Harcourt had the reversion of the Liberal leadership,[8] and that Sir William's idea of Home Rule was Mr Joseph Chamberlain's system of local government. He declared in that smoking-room to me – and I think Mr Henry Campbell, the present Town Clerk of Dublin was present – that if Sir William Harcourt came into position and power he would give Ireland local government and plenty of coercion; that he knew what Mr Gladstone would do, having had it at Hawarden from his own lips; that he knew what Mr John Morley was inclined to do, but that there was not a single one of the lot to be 'trusted'. All through that crisis Mr Parnell, hot from a stormy and excited meeting, preserved the most remarkable frigidity of demeanour and countenance, and the calmest and precisest speech. He drank coffee and smoked a small cigar, which he seemed to have a store of, for it was always the same brand. He seemed quite happy in offering his friends a smoke, but rarely suggested drink. Still hock was his ordinary dinner wine – Nierstein or Hockheim – and though he rarely if ever quoted poetry, he would drily recite a distich of Longfellow's, recounting where were grown the three best kinds of wine. Walt Whitman, also an American poet, was the only other writer of verse whom he appeared to relish. I heard him on a memorable occasion quote with great effect the lines ending 'it might have been',[9] and who does not recollect the famous speech when he

20

misquoted the familiar verse:, 'First flower of the earth', and as he put it, with some hesitation, 'First gem of the "ocean".'[10]

Mr Davitt was always carping at Mr Parnell. He believed him to have filched his kudos of fathership of the Land League. Yet I never heard Mr Parnell say any unkind word of Mr Davitt; but, on the contrary, I have heard him express the greatest sympathy for Mr Davitt, as a man a great slice of whose life was, so to speak, cut out in his prime in prison. I remember when Mr Davitt made the declaration that 'the cause of Home Rule was not only dead, but,' added he, 'if you will permit me to say so, damned for twelve years at least.' Parnell's comment on the saying was: 'I am curious to know how Davitt arrived at the calculation of twelve years; it is not his habit to be accurate.' This was the period when Mr Davitt desired the Irish Leadership to be put in commission, 'the members to be Messrs Justin McCarthy, John Dillon, Thomas Sexton, Timothy Healy – and probably himself'.

On the night after Mr Timothy Healy grossly insulted Mr Parnell – a night in December, when he accused him of having suffocated the alliance with the Liberal Party of England in the stench of the Divorce Court – Mr Parnell supped in the grill-room of the Grand Hotel, near Charing Cross, and discussing the scene that had taken place, he said to me and others – Mr Richard Power, late member for Waterford, was one – that upon the introduction of the Home Rule Bill of 1886 he called a number of his party together and told them that they should share the responsibilities of the situation with him; that he had a message to give them to the effect that if they did not accept the Bill as it stood the Cabinet would resign in a body, and that he would not throw away such an opportunity. They should either take the Bill or wreck the Ministry! They agreed to accept the Bill, although vital matters like the Land Question, the Judiciary, and the Control of the Constabulary were reserved cases – made so by Mr Gladstone. That was the evening of the day upon which Mr Parnell said he would stand or fall by his version of the negotiations with the Liberal Party, whereupon Mr Healy shouted: 'Then you will fall!' They were stormy times, and full of sentiment, sensation, and slanging. One MP – I forget which side of the fray he took – declared that 'those with him were the brains of the party, not its brogues'; and Mr Healy declared that he derided the authority of Mr Parnell, and appealed against it, and that 'the heads of greater leaders had been stricken on the block before now'. This was the man of whom he had said a short time before, in the Leinster Hall, 'He is less a man than an institution,' and called upon the people 'not to speak to the man at the wheel.'

Sir Parnell.

I have already narrated how I accompanied Mr Parnell to Hawarden, and, although I did not stay at the Castle, as he did, but returned to Chester, where Mr Parnell dined with me previous to our setting forth for the Liverpool Reform Club, I heard him afterwards say that in his four hours conference with Mr Gladstone, 'the garrulous old man' told him that in his opinion, and in that of his colleagues, the Irish representation in Parliament should be reduced from 103 members to 32; that the Land Question must be reserved from the control of the Irish Legislature; that the Irish Constabulary should remain under Imperial control for an indefinite period, and that the appointment of judges and resident magistrates must be kept in the hands of the Imperial authority for ten or twelve years.

On the same occasion he mentioned to me that Mr John Morley had suggested that he should become Chief Secretary, and that a legal member of the party should be made a law officer of the Crown. As a matter of fact, Mr Parnell never intended to join the Irish government, but rather aimed at being Home Secretary for England, whence he could guide it, and possibly Prime Minister, for after the exposure and suicide of Pigott, the collapse of the *Times* Commission, and his own complete vindication, Mr Parnell was unmistakably one of the

22

most powerful, if not one of the most popular politicians in England.

He had been hunted and hounded down. I, on more than one occasion, crossed in the mail boats during the period when he was regarded with so much suspicion and dread. He was in wretched health, and had all the seeming of a pursued person. He usually occupied the fore cabin and his identity was kept as dark as possible. His name never appeared on the ship's register, and his movements were shrouded in mystery. After all the passengers had got off the steamer and into their trains and when the luggage had been taken ashore, a tall wan figure, with unkempt beard and hair, and badly dressed, but yet significantly distinguished looking, would emerge from below and stride across the platform to a carriage, the door of which was held open for him by a porter. This was Parnell, and few of the passengers either on boat or train ever knew of his presence. It is quite true that he used aliases, and kept his addresses secret, save from those with whom it was absolutely necessary to keep in touch.

Mr Parnell always referred to his American tour in 1880 with a shiver, and he regarded it as a nightmare, notwithstanding its signal success.

He was at his best in his own house of Avondale or a big night in the House of Commons. His presence, manner, and genial personality seemed to fascinate both members and visitors, and when he was there he was the cynosure of all eyes. His speech was rare, restrained, and in every way reserved. They hung, however, on his words, and as sure as he made a suggestive utterance, something startling was certain to follow in the country. It was a sight to see Mr Gladstone, who looked on Mr Parnell as one of the most remarkable personages of the century, albeit neither liked the other, watching the Irish leader and placing himself in his latter-day characteristic attitude and posture, with hand behind his ear, drinking in Mr Parnell's nervous, measured, and vigorous sentences when a pronouncement had to be made.

I asked one day, when I was travelling alone with him from Holyhead to London, 'why public men are so vain'. It was not any act of his which prompted me to put the query, and I cannot at the present moment recall for those random recollections what had; but I remember distinctly clear-cut reply: 'Out of the necessity of the case, sir', said he, addressing me by my name.[11]

For Mr Morley, Mr Parnell entertained a kind of pitying respect, if not regard. 'There he is now,' said he, at a crucial epoch of his own declining career, 'sitting out at Killiney, twirling his thumbs and muttering to himself, "What can I do?"'[12] The event justified the description, and revealed the penetration of Parnell.

During the progress of the *Times* Special Commission I had frequent interviews with Mr Parnell. I remember that in conversation he was always particularly severe on W.H. Smith[13] and Mr Walter.[14] He characterized the conduct of the former as abominable, and used to say that Mr Smith had fallen into very bad company when he had a visit from, and was led astray by, Mr Walter. With regard to the famous or infamous letters, he constantly reiterated to me that he had not written them, and that he and Mr Labouchere[15] knew who had, but that he would allow his accusers to 'fool themselves to the top of their bent'. He also declared in the presence of me and others that he did not care a brass farthing about their finding on any other matters – which he crisply grouped as 'general accusations'.

He also seemed to have a particular aversion to Mr Chamberlain and he relished exceedingly a statement or sneer made by, I think, Mr Labouchere, already mentioned, who described Mr Chamberlain as roving about introducing a herd of members of his family and himself to members of the aristocracy, and who added that the head, sons, brothers, and brothers-in-law of the Chamberlain tribe reminded one of those troupes of acrobats that travelled about and that were advertized on the bills as 'patronized by the nobility and gentry'. This tickled Mr Parnell very much. It was a caustic saying of which he might himself have been the author.

About Lord Hartington,[16] I never heard him say anything harsh; but he complained, I can recall, of a speech made by the present Duke of Devonshire as making an unfair blow or thrust, when he represented to the English people that after the then generation of Irish leaders had passed away, Irishmen would not be content to accept permanently a position in the world inferior to that which they held, namely, remaining in Parliament to vote upon all subjects. What Mr Parnell particularly took umbrage at was the innuendo by Lord Hartington that England would be entirely excluded from all control over the internal affairs of Ireland, but that Irishmen would remain at Westminster to settle the fate of England and Scotland, and that the inevitable alternative was that Ireland would claim complete separation. Mr Parnell regarded this as a perverted version of the subject. For Lord Randolph Churchill he either felt or affected regard, especially for his baiting of the 'Grand Old Man', for whom Mr Parnell seemed to have no genuine respect. He laughed heartily – and his laugh was very rare, though he had a most cheery and genial smile – at one expression of Randolph's, who had said that 'the only paupers in Ireland were "the Irish landlords"'. Lord Randolph about this period made almost a prophetic forecast which Mr Parnell, I suppose, seeing in his mystic way the shadows before of coming events, took to heart. It was something like this:

Mr Gladstone [said his assailant] has seen three Irish parties come into being, apparently powerful. He saw the party led by Mr O'Connell. He saw the Irish Brigade, or the 'Pope's Brass Band'. He saw the numerically stronger party under the leadership of Mr Butt. They all broke up, and disappeared in Mr Gladstone's own time, in consequence of internecine discord, and everything I observe in the party of Mr Parnell leads me to the conclusion that this hereditary discord, tending towards paralysis and the shattering of the party, exists at present.

Mr Parnell was himself much struck by that forecast based on history, and so soon destined to be realized.

Mr Parnell was constitutionally adverse to *ad captandum* or transient rhetoric. In this respect he differed essentially from Lord Randolph Churchill, who was a rash and reckless, though a clever speaker.

If I were asked to say offhand what virtue Mr Parnell respected in the highest degree I think I should answer manliness. He certainly did say that no Englishman had any respect for an Irishman, until the said Irishman knocked him down.

This actually occurred in his own career, for at Cambridge Mr Parnell, stung by some taunt at his nationality, did actually hit out and bowled over the aggressor, with whom, it is on record, he afterwards became fast and firm friends.

Towards clerics of all persuasions, Mr Parnell presented a stiff front. Perhaps he had a presentiment that they would be instrumental in his downfall. He was not always judicious in this attitude, and at one era gravely offended an archbishop,[17] by avoiding meeting him, after entering into engagements through his private secretary to have an interview with him in London. These were the days of the plan of campaign, and perhaps the exigencies of the position, rather than aversion to the ecclesiastical, compelled Mr Parnell's conduct. The dignitary referred to never forgot, if he forgave, the incident, and was foremost in taking sides against Mr Parnell and demanding his retirement.

Parnell was fond of quoting a phrase used to his ancestor, Sir John Parnell, Chancellor of the Irish Exchequer before the Union, by a Catholic prelate, to the effect that he would rather have a union with the Beys and Mamelukes of Egypt than be under the iron rod of the Mamelukes of Ireland. Mr Parnell held that the Catholics desired to escape from under the control of the 'Mamelukes of the Ascendancy Parliament'.

I was present when a discussion took place one night on how to keep a party together, and was greatly struck by a remark made by Mr Parnell, who interjected that Palmerston stuck to his subordinates through thick and through thin; but that Bismarck dismissed his on the complaint of the most commonplace. I can recall Mr Parnell ironically alluding to Mr Courtney,[18] who said the things that would be entrusted to a county council in Ireland would be probably restricted at first to the care of roads. Mr Parnell grimly commented: 'I wonder would he give us any control over the pigs that are constantly wandering on them', and wondering at the constabulary, over whom Mr Courtney had said 'nobody would dream of giving Ireland control', though in England the county councils had half control over the police, the constables being, before the Local Government Act, a county affair.

Of Sir Richard Webster, then Attorney General for England, and who conducted the case for *The Times* against him, Mr Parnell had a poor opinion, and he laughed at a speech delivered by Sir Richard, who wanted to know would Local Government satisfy such men as Mr Parnell and Mr Davitt.

Mr Parnell liked to be reminded of and to discuss that speech of Lord Beaconsfield's, familiarly known as 'the ape and the angel' speech, in which the master of gibes, flouts and sneers scoffed at 'nebulous professors, the perusal of whose writings is a foretaste of that eternal punishment which they affect to disbelieve'.

For himself, however, he rarely, if ever, used inflated language, though his style was singularly strong. At a memorable election in Louth he did let out on Mr Philip Callan,[19] and his rhetoric was sharp and stingy. One phrase he used was almost brutal in its application. He said: 'If you let a hog swim long enough it will cut its own throat'; but of language such as used in the *United Ireland*[20] of the time, he did not approve. He objected in conversation to the phraseology in which Lord Spencer[21] was dubbed 'Foxey Jack'. Mr Balfour was called 'brutal, beastly, blackguard and bloody', and a 'detestable, despicable, and dastardly despot', as well as a 'fraudulent and flippant liar', and a 'malignant, malicious, miserable

Mr. Parnell turns his back on Public Opinion.

murderer'. He had a contempt for Sir George Trevelyan,[22] but he expressed disapproval of his being called 'the meanest creature that ever crawled upon the earth'. He said it was true the press was not free but that 'scurrility would not bring it freedom'.

In his own language, both in the way it was couched and the words employed, he was a thorough gentleman. He had some very quaint sayings; one, whether it was his own originally or

27

not I cannot say, made a lasting impression on me: 'A big man', remarked he, 'requires a big horse to ride, not two small horses.'

Mr Parnell took the greatest interest in scientific subjects and, like Lord Salisbury, spent much of his time in a laboratory. He was also greatly interested in the cutting of the Manchester Ship Canal, and in the works begun outside Boulogne, with the object of boring a tunnel beneath the Channel between England and France. His reading was not diffuse, but it was accurate, and his retention of what he read remarkable.

In 1880 somebody of little or no account wrote to Mr Gladstone asking him one of those extraordinary questions which, it passed into a phrase, invariably fetched a postcard from the veteran statesman. It ran something like this: 'Is it possible to dispense with the Irish members at Westminster and yet retain Ireland as an integral part of the United Kingdom, as at present, without coercing at the same time loyal Ulster?' Whereupon the GOM[23] dispatched the customary postcard to his correspondent, which was to the following effect:

The answer to your question is contained in the Home Rule Bill of 1886, which showed my belief that my withdrawal of the Irish members involved no danger to the Empire; in the state of things before 1800, when, without Irishmen at Westminster, the Empire was perhaps quite as united as now; but, if the country wishes it otherwise, I think it ought to be otherwise, and the Irish members should remain.

Mr Parnell, after reading this characteristic effusion, quietly commented: 'Mr Gladstone's supply of postcards ought to be cut off.'

Mr Parnell was very specific in classifying the shades of opinion and the complexion of parties in Parliament. He frequently said, discussing the attitude of the British Parliament with regard to Ireland, that there were three distinct and different policies for the treatment of this country; the first creating a statutory Parliament and Executive for the control of Ireland's domestic affairs; the second conceding some form of local government; thirdly, the maintenance of the *status quo*, to be ultimately modified by municipal and local self-government. He, at the period of which I write, more than a year before the split, counted the bulk of the Liberal Party as pledged to the first-named; Lord Randolph Churchill, Mr Chamberlain, some members of the government, and some of the Conservative rank and file to the second; and the Marquis of Salisbury, the Marquis of Hartington (now Duke of Devonshire), with the mass of the Liberal Unionists to the third.

I saw him greatly irritated once by the remarks made in his presence that the British Liberal Party was being wagged by its tail – the Irish Party. He vehemently and indignantly denied that the Irish Parliamentary Party was the tail of any English party, or that they stood under what was called at the time the 'grand old umbrella'. He was highly amused indeed when someone of the Tories, I think the generally sedate Sir Michael Hicks Beach, likened the Irish treatment of Mr Gladstone to that accorded by certain savage tribes to their idols when they do not grant their prayers – 'give them a sound drubbing'. For Lord Aberdeen,[24] Mr Parnell had apparently a sincere regard, and of a speech of whose, dissipating the contention that Home Rule would jeopardize or damage Protestantism in Ireland, he more than once spoke highly, as having an excellent effect in England and Scotland. Someone compared himself to one of the hairs of the Liberal tail, a fantasy by which the Irish leader felt exceedingly tickled. One of his axioms was that England could never have the use of her own Parliament till she had settled the Irish question, and though he was fond of 'Gallant Little Wales', he always insisted that before Disestablishment in the Principality, Home Rule should be established in Ireland.

Mr Parnell never cordially approved of the Plan of Campaign, and, indeed, he did not put a tooth upon plainly saying so in a railway carriage to the present writer. The condition of the evicted tenants and the wreck of the fine homes of Old Tipperary Town, and the mistake of New Tipperary,[25] gave him trouble and pain. He had a singularly fine touch, and not even the spectacle of English audiences cheering for 'The Plan' deceived him.

Mr Parnell's connection with Mr Patrick Egan,[26] who, it was alleged, had become a member of the Clan na Gael, when alluded to during the *Times* Commission, evoked the remark that if Egan had become a Mormon, he, Parnell, could not be held responsible for that. Besides, Egan was held in such estimation by the United States government that they appointed him their Minister in Chile.

When Mr Parnell was in America it used to be said of him, as a proof of his popularity and wide-spreading fame, that if a letter were addressed with no other superscription on it than 'Parnell, America', it would reach him, and that the same would happen if he were in Asia: 'Parnell, Asia', would find him there too.

I was present many times when Mr Parnell was before the judges or rather, the Special Commission,[27] Sir James Hannen, Mr Justice Day, and Mr Justice Smith. He used to be highly amused at the vacant expression on the face of Judge Day, who was notable for never uttering a word and wearing the blankest aspect. Mr Parnell's demeanour throughout was one of impassive indifference, although he preserved a respectful and decorous dignity before his judges. The 'last link' speech, as it was called, was delivered in Cincinnati,[28] but considerable doubt was thrown upon whether Mr Parnell ever used the words. He was notoriously careless about the reports of his speeches, and after the Attorney-General had pressed home the point against him, I remember Mr Davitt speaking and protesting against Sir Richard Webster so emphasizing a garbled extract from a newspaper published in another hemisphere, while alleging for himself that he had been working almost all his life to break the last link that bound Ireland to England under present circumstances, and to substitute for that link, a link of friendship and mutual understanding and confidence. As a matter of memory, I was present in the House of Commons when, in reply to a taunt of Sir George Trevelyan, Mr Parnell repudiated the 'last link' sentiment. As somebody said at the time, it was as fair to hold Mr Parnell responsible for the 'maxims for skirmishers' in *The Irish World* – Mr Ford's organ[29] – as it would be to call the Tory Chancellor of the Exchequer a Home Ruler because he received millions of pounds in taxes from those advocating and voting for Home Rule.

Mr Parnell was very nervous as to the doings of the Ladies'

Land League, and his own sister[30] brought to the leading Nationalist daily of which I was editor, a letter attacking him in no measured language. I remonstrated with her, and endeavoured to dissuade her from seeking its publication. With true Parnell pertinacity she argued the matter for hours through the night, when eventually I prevailed and she consented to withdraw the manuscript. I never had a keener controversy in my life than with that lady, who resembles her great brother in many respects, mentally as well as facially.

Mr Parnell was an excellent statistician and would have made a splendid and superb Chancellor of the Exchequer. I have a memorandum in my possession, jotted down during a conversation with him after the starting of the Land League in Mayo. He was talking about the impoverished condition of the country, and he said offhand that in 1841 there were in Mayo 68,425 inhabited houses, and that the population numbered 387,887. Less than 40 years having elapsed, the number of inhabited houses fell to 42,458 and the people had dwindled to 245,212. Now, said Mr Parnell, estimating at #100 each a person's value to the country, the loss incurred in this way in Mayo alone would not be much less than #20,000,000 without counting at all the value of the inhabited houses which had disappeared in the meantime. Mr Davitt made a similar statement. *The Times* wrote that every workingman in England had an Irish peasant on his back, and may deem himself only too fortunate if both are not floundering in the mud before next August.

Mr Chamberlain once said that Coercion was only a nickname, and meant merely the carrying out of the ordinary law. 'He has never been in prison', drily observed Mr Parnell. Mr Parnell had himself chafed very much under his incarceration in Kilmainham, and always exhibited the keenest sympathy with political offenders in confinement. At the period of which I now write, Mr Chamberlain was enkindling the fires of sectarian bigotry as well as race hatred between England and Ireland, provoking from Mr John Morley the severest rebuke when he asked an English audience:

What would you think of an Irishman who went down among his brother Catholics and recalled to them the laws which the Protestants

31

made against the Catholics – laws which gave bribes to the Protestant wife to inform against her Catholic husband, bribes to the Protestant child for informing against his Catholic father, which deprived Catholics of every chance of advancement, and of which it was truly said that it was a code devised not merely to exterminate a religious sect, but to degrade a nation, to plant the foot of foreign conquerors on the backs of the people, to quench every instinct that is good, to deprive them of every right which freemen can claim, and which remains as one of the blackest pages in the history of religious persecution? I should say that the Irish Catholic who did this would be guilty of a heinous offence, and I say that the English Protestant who tries to enkindle Protestant bigotry is also guilty of a heinous offence.

A late Protestant Archbishop of Dublin, speaking in Dublin about the same time, declared that the chief danger to be apprehended in Dublin was not the ascendancy of a hostile Church, but the prevalence of anarchical and socialistic doctrines. Mr Lecky, one of the sitting members for Trinity, himself a Liberal Unionist, as well as an historian, also showed that Mr Chamberlain was false in his facts and foul in his language.

Mr Parnell was delighted at all this, and did not conceal the pleasure he experienced at Mr Chamberlain's chastisement. His hopes were high at the time. The case, 'Parnellism and Crime', set up against him by *The Times*, had crumbled to atoms under the touchstone of truth, applied to it with such effect by the present Lord Chief Justice of England, the Catholic Lord Russell of Killowen. Alas! Within little more than a year the favourite of the hour was himself felled by the hypocrisy of the Nonconformist Conscience, and the instability and treachery of his own Irish followers!

When Mr Davitt went to America Mr Parnell was not aware of it, and was not consulted by him, though in the trial before the *Times* Commission it was sought to couple or bracket them, and connect Mr Parnell with Fenianism and treasonable conspiracy. Mr Davitt himself, to his credit be it said, cleared up this matter in his defence, and after completely exonerating Mr Parnell, clinched the matter, and nailed the lie by averring that he went to America to see his family, and the only member of Parliament he met there was Mr James J. O'Kelly!

There were two very distinct negotiations between eminent members of the Tory Party and the Irish leaders. The first of

ERIN AT THE BIER OF PARNELL.

Supplement Gratis with "UNITED IRELAND." 6th October, 1894.

them took place in 1885, when the Liberal Party was in power
and when a secret understanding was arrived at between the
Irish leaders and the Tory leaders. The story went that, in return
for the support of the Irish Party, in turning out the Liberal
government, the Tory leaders promised to oppose the renewal
of the Coercion Act. Sir H. Drummond Wolff[31] was unquestionably an intermediary in this transaction. It was stated at the
time that the question of Home Rule was actually discussed and
voted upon in Lord Salisbury's Cabinet of 1885. The differences
of opinion on the subject were more probably settled outside
the Cabinet, and it appears to be now admitted that they led to
the resignation of Lord Carnarvon. There is little or no doubt
that the implication of the Marquis of Salisbury in the history of
the Home Rule transactions stood upon his appointment of
Lord Carnarvon as Lord Lieutenant of Ireland, and his
knowledge of Lord Carnarvon's negotiations with Mr Parnell
and his Newport speech. I may premise, that it was considered
at the time, in view of the great change which was then
impending in the Irish representation that it would be the duty
of whatever party may be in power after the election, to endeavour to come to an arrangement with the Irish Party for an
alteration in this government of Ireland.

I will state now my personal recollection of Lord Carnarvon's
connection with the matter. The Earl Lord-Lieutenant of Ireland
was an elderly gentleman, amiable of disposition, and well
disposed in every way. I happened to be in a restaurant, I think
Hynes's of Dame Street, one day, and I was addressed by a
Scotchman, a merchant tailor, who said to me, 'I saw a friend of
yours at the Viceregal Lodge yesterday.' Without attaching any
moment to the remark or circumstance, I said: 'Pray, who was
he?' 'Well,' my acquaintance replied, 'he was no less a
gentleman than Edmund Dwyer Gray.'[32] 'I think you must be
mistaken, sir,' I rejoined, 'because Mr Gray does not go to the
Castle or to the Lodge.' He repeated smilingly: 'I know him
very well, and I saw him go into luncheon with the Countess of
Carnarvon, and what is more, I saw Mrs Gray go into luncheon
with the Lord-Lieutenant.' The gentleman is still young and
prospering in this city at present, and he may contradict me if I

am recording anything in error. Mrs O'Connor, then Mrs Gray, is also living and youthful, and she may have the opportunity of correcting me if the story be a mistaken one, or if my remembrance be defective. 'What, may I ask, brought you into their company or to the Lodge?' I said. 'Well,' he replied, in somewhat broad Scotch, 'I, as perhaps you know, am a tailor, and I was favoured with an order to go to the Viceregal Lodge to have liveries made for the lackeys, and while I was there I saw, as much to my own astonishment as to yours, Mr Gray as I describe.' I still had some hesitation or doubt about the matter, but I took the earliest opportunity of seeing Mr Gray in his newspaper room. 'Sir,' I said, 'I have heard a most extraordinary story about you. I heard you have been lunching with Lord Carnarvon.' He appeared quite surprised, and even startled, and said to me, 'Who told you that?' I detailed to him the story as it was told to me. He enjoined me with emphasis not to repeat it, but he did not deny its accuracy.

It was on that occasion that the interview with Mr Parnell was arranged[33] as I have been since informed, and that the Tory Viceroy and the Irish leader met secretly. There was a characteristic comment in *The Times* about that period, or, perhaps, some years after, to the effect that

it was a curious method of reasoning to make Lord Salisbury responsible for all the changes in Lord Carnarvon's mind, and adding that, on the same principles, it could be proved that Lord Palmerston was in favour of Home Rule, because Mr Gladstone long before his 'perversion', was his Chancellor of the Exchequer.

It went on to say that Lord Carnarvon was known to be somewhat of a sentimentalist, and to have a strong belief in Federalism as a 'political panacea'.

Mr Parnell was as keenly alive to the exigencies of the highland crofter as he was to those of the Irish peasant. There was a Mr Donald McFarlane, a member of Parliament in those days, who took a great interest in the Crofter Question. An island called Lewis, of about half a million acres had, at the time of which I write, about half of it preserved for sporting purposes some of which had been formed, or transformed, into deer forests from lands occupied by crofters and cottiers. A lady (Matheson, I think, was the name) was the proprietress, and, so well as my memory serves, some hundreds of those cottiers waited on her to petition that portions of the land kept uncultivated should be divided amongst the poor people. Her reply was: 'When you cannot pay for the land which you have, how can you pay for more? Sell your stock, pay your rent, and earn a living out of your fishing.' The answer was that, owing to the want of a fishing harbour and other accessories to a fishing industry, they could not fish, and if they sold their stock the proceeds would not pay one year's rent, and then they would have nothing. The alternative proposed to them was: 'Then you should go to foreign lands.' When Mr Parnell heard of this, or it was brought under his notice in the press, he pithily said: 'A Frenchman once advised his countrymen to eat grass if they could not get bread', and he sardonically finished that the man himself set an example, for some time after his mouth was found full of grass. I give this as an example of his grimness. He held the theory that a long line of monarchs gave away to private individuals that which was not theirs to give – the land of these islands – and that the system supported by venal Parliament ended in the deprivation of the people of much that was theirs by right.

A capital cartoon, and one which created considerable commotion, appeared in *United Ireland* at a juncture when Mr Parnell instituted proceedings in Scotland – in Edinburgh – against *The Times*. Under Scottish law, an action may be instituted against any outsider possessing property in that country. Money for newspapers was due *The Times* by three Edinburgh firms, and upon each of these Mr Parnell had writs served, and the cartoon referred to represented him in deadly conflict with *The Times* in bonnie Scotland over an apt adaptation of a version from 'The Lady of the Lake':

'Now man to man and steel to steel
A chieftain's vengeance thou shalt feel.'[34]

At the same juncture Mr John E. Redmond and other members of Parliament – Mr T.P. O'Connor, I think, was one - instituted actions against 'the thunderer'.

Mr Chamberlain, who feared Mr Parnell, and was jealous of

him, produced about this period a scheme for the establishment of County Boards in Ireland, which he alleged as given to him by Captain O'Shea, with the sanction of Mr Parnell. The whole figment tumbled like a house of cards for Chamberlain failed to produce an atom or iota of proof that the Irish leader had anything to do with the affair at all, while every act of his political life went to prove that he couldn't have had anything to say to it. In point of fact, in a letter to *The Times*, which had stated on Mr Chamberlain's authority that his scheme of local government for Ireland had not only Mr Parnell's approval, but that it could be proven out of his own handwriting and over his own signature, Mr Parnell challenged Mr Chamberlain, if he possessed such proofs, to produce them. Mr Chamberlain, if my memory of the transaction does not fail me, accepted the challenge; but in a letter written almost immediately afterwards he wrote – 'The idea was never at any time worked out in detail, and it was not the subject of any discourse with Mr O'Shea. I am, consequently, quite ready', he added, 'to admit Mr Parnell's disclaimer of any assent to it.' Was there ever such a collapse? The contemptuous smile which passed over Mr Parnell's habitually impassible countenance was a treat to witness when he read Mr Chamberlain's come-down. It was in this correspondence that he repudiated Captain O'Shea as a 'go between' as he termed it.[35] This was not the only withdrawal Mr Chamberlain had to make about the time, for he had also alleged that all the leading citizens of America were adverse to Home Rule. He was promptly contradicted by several of them, and all that he could reply in extenuation of his language was that they were adverse to Mr Gladstone's methods of policy.

POSTSCRIPT: PARNELL
AND THE PRESS

The rise of Parnellism was intimately bound up with the emergence of a popular press in Ireland and England. The Parnellite movement was a triumph of propaganda, as well as of political leadership and mobilization. Harold Frederic, the London correspondent of *The New York Times*, estimated in 1887 that over one-sixth of the Irish Party were themselves working journalists. The political initiation of most of the leadership of the party occurred through journalism: in particular T.M. Healy, William O'Brien, Justin McCarthy, T.P. O'Connor, Thomas Sexton. They were skilled and resourceful combatants in the propaganda war which was the Irish Question in late Victorian politics.[1]

The myth of Parnell was refracted through the contemporary press. If his 'chieftaincy' was a product of Irish circumstances alone, Parnell was also, in his way, the first media celebrity of modern politics. Acclaimed and ostensibly revered by his countrymen, Parnell was the inscrutable and elusive Irish leader, 'the mystery man', given a sinister glamour by the aura of Fenian violence with which he was invested in English press perception. His fall was sensational, eclipsing in political consequence that of Sir Charles Dilke in 1886, and achieving a notoriety comparable to the conviction of Oscar Wilde in 1895.

The exceedingly clever Healy, who had been the first journalistic propagandist of Parnellism, seized the opportunity presented by the split to pay himself a back-handed compliment, and to push the argument of a press-driven myth one stage further. He shrewdly observed that the leader's political image was shaped as much by the anti-nationalist English newspapers as by the nationalist press in Ireland, and those other 'hostile journalists who pursued him at the outset of his career as a bore, a blunderer, and a petulant', who 'wheeled

39

around later on to invest his successes with unfathomable accompaniments of mystery and surprise'. He further argued that Parnell had himself been seduced by his own myth. He regarded the leader as so shallow a personality, and so indeterminate and passively opportunistic a politician, that the lineaments of his character bore the impress of the cult surrounding him:

He has been largely created not only by himself and his colleagues, but by his enemies. He has been moulded too in a sort of English matrix. When he did not appear in the House of Commons, and the Tory press got out stories of his mysterious disappearances, and referred to him as the one solitary man wrapping his cloak around him like Napoleon at St Helena, or as the one strong man defying and despising everybody else, he, of course, read these things, and, as Oscar Wilde put it, lived up to the level of his blue china.[2]

Parnell maintained close relations, not just with Edward Byrne and James M. Tuohy of the *Freeman's Journal*, but with Alfred Robbins, the lobby correspondent of the *Birmingham Daily Post*, and his brother-in-law Ernest W. Pitt, of *The Times* and the Press Association. Robbins was, as he put it, 'in intimate and frequent confidence with Parnell during the last four years of his life'. His London correspondence for his paper attested to his close knowledge of the political thinking of the Irish leader.

In *Parnell, The Last Five Years*, Robbins portrayed the Irish leader as a disarmingly candid figure, anxious above all to rein in the excesses of the nationalist movement in the prelude to Home Rule. The lobby system, of which Robbins was an early practitioner, was in its infancy, but Parnell's relations with Robbins were part of a more complex traffic of influences than a formalized arrangement for confidential briefings.[3]

Parnell trusted Robbins' discretion and confidentiality:

In a lull in one Lobby conversation, he broodingly looked at me, and suddenly said, 'Robbins, do you know why I trust you so absolutely?' The question did not admit of easy reply, but, scarcely pausing, he himself supplied the answer, 'Because you never leak.' I lived my journalistic life striving to continue deserving the highest compliment a Lobbyist, as I conceived him, could have paid . . .[4]

Robbins recalled walking with Parnell up and down the Embankment between Westminster and Charing Cross, conversing at a length which would have attracted attention in the Lobby:

Despite the extreme reticence he was accustomed to display in conversation, he would talk with great freedom to anyone who had won his
confidence. During the four years of our frequent intercourse, at times
of great moment to himself personally as well as to his public career, I
never found him anything but perfectly courteous, and some-times
strangely communicative.

Recalling Parnell as he had known him, at the height of his
power, and the depth of his fall, Robbins testified to 'his un-
varying straightforwardness to myself, even in times of great
difficulty, when a diplomatic deception might have served him
well'.[5]

The affection Robbins and Pitt had for Parnell did not
impinge on their journalistic independence; Robbins recalled
that when Pitt returned from covering the North Kilkenny
election, in which Parnell had forfeited his former poise, 'he
mournfully told me "he's not the Parnell you and I have known.
That Parnell is dead"'.[6]

Robbins was alive to the political irony: 'Strangely enough he
fully trusted only two English journalists – my brother-in-law
Pitt and myself – and it's the more strange in my case as I
represented a newspaper absolutely opposed to his policy.'[7]
Parnell could not rely on the exclusive embrace of pro-Home
Rule Liberal press, whose primary allegiance was owed to
Gladstone. Throughout the critical phase 1886-90, Parnell, while
upholding the Liberal-Nationalist alliance, sought unremit-
tingly to maximize his freedom of action within it. His relations
with Robbins defied the prevalent perception that he was the
captive or, what was much the same thing, the captor of the
Liberal alliance. He thereby signalled his determination to
maintain his access to those outside its ranks. He sought to
evade the tightening alignment of British politics around the
issue of Home Rule, and the attendant hardening of his own
image. His relations with Robbins were part of that determined
thwarting of expectations which was so characteristic of his
political technique: he must have used the journalist as a
sounding-board, and Robbins probably served as the Irish
leader's eyes and ears during a period when illness frequently

41

kept him from parliament, helping him to divine the drift of thinking within the Liberal Unionist camp.

Parnell won a high level of personal respect and even affection among journalists; he treated them with a lack of affectation or condescension that belied the fabled severity of his House of Commons demeanour. He proved thus to be in advance of his English contemporaries as a practitioner of modern democratic politics. While the attention of contemporary English political leaders was largely absorbed in endeavouring to influence susceptible newspaper editors and proprietors, Parnell felt an evident affinity with the pressmen who covered his speeches and campaigns. They were fellow political professionals with whom he shared a certain *esprit de corps*. He welcomed their company to mitigate the rigours and the isolation of political campaigning, which popular acclaim could not dispel.

The only occasion on which J. M. Tuohy saw Parnell lose his temper with a journalist was when, on learning that W. T. Stead of the *Pall Mall Gazette* was encroaching on his investigation into the provenance of the Pigott forgeries, he snapped at a representative of the paper: 'In God's name, why does not Mr Stead occupy himself with his own affairs and cease his intermeddling with those of other people who don't need his assistance?'[8]

Writing a year after Parnell's death, an unnamed 'Irish Reporter' recalled Parnell as exceptionally considerate to the journalists who covered his meetings. They fell under the sway of 'the singular fascination of his manner': 'Personally, who like Mr Parnell realised so thoroughly the troubles and difficulties of the pressman? Who, like him, so completely ignored any considerations of political exigency when dealing with the representative of a newspaper?' To journalists he repeatedly instanced kindness.

To no class of men was there afforded a better opportunity of knowing Mr Parnell intimately than to Irish pressmen. Sunday after Sunday they had to travel long distances with him in trains, and on cars and wagonettes and, believe me, there is no better means of arriving at a proper and truthful diagnosis of the man.

They had no experience of Parnell's supposedly cold demeanour: 'To meet him after a wearying day's demonstration, when many a man might be excused for wrapping himself up in a cloak of coldness and apathy, was a revelation of his better nature.'

When his speech at a banquet in Limerick went unreported because the journalists withdrew in protest at the inadequacy of the facilities afforded them, Parnell took care to express

his appreciation of our action, for, as he said, the amiability of reporters had too often led them to accept the most inadequate accommodation, and the most indifferent regard for their convenience, rather than complain.

Parnell's solicitude extended even to the police on a rather different occasion. He averted the risk of a riot at Castlerea, where it had been resolved to exclude government note-takers from the meeting. When the police began to force their way through the crowd, Parnell said to the officer in charge that the note-takers could come to the front of the platform: 'I will be responsible for their safety and protection on condition that you remove all your men to the barracks and keep them out of view, and there will be no disturbance.'

The striking concision of Parnell's speeches, which eschewed the habitual prolixity of nationalist oratory, owed much to the need to ensure their accurate and effective reporting. Of his earlier speeches, the 'Irish Reporter' noted:

He adopted the system of never speaking more than would make about the ordinary column of a newspaper, and over and over again when the enthusiastic plaudits of a crowd or the vehemence of a reception accorded to him might well have tempted him to prolong a speech he would just give that column and no more. One result of this was it developed that method of epigrammatic condensation which made his utterance so strikingly effective and another that he was sure to get a perfectly satisfactory report, for that column was invariably good 'copy', acceptable to every paper, and expressed in such a way as to make it a pleasure to report or read it.[9]

It may be surmised that Irish pressmen played an unobserved role in keeping Parnell in touch with popular opinion in Ireland, and that he lost the benefit of their counsel in the long hiatus between the Galway election of February 1886 and

December 1890, during which he did not speak in Ireland. Between the split and his death, 1890-1, Parnell campaigned ceaselessly in Ireland, and was again thrown into the company of Irish journalists.

After his Kilkenny defeat, on the Christmas Eve of 1890, Parnell visited his iron mines with a *Freeman's Journal* reporter he had not met before, and discussed the history of the locality and the mines, making no allusion whatever to politics.[10]

On the train to his last meeting at Creggs, Parnell asked the two journalists of the *Freeman's Journal* to join him in his carriage, and protected them from the ire of his supporters at the meeting. One of them, Russell, recalled: 'He was very ill and suffered much pain, but he talked all the way and would not let me sleep.'[11]

NOTES

INTRODUCTION

1. The biographical information on Byrne is derived principally from press obituaries: *Irish Daily Independent*, 14 Oct. 1899; *Evening Herald*, 13 Oct. 1899; *Cork Examiner*, 14 Oct. 1899; *Tuam Herald*, 20 Oct. 1899. The most extended obituary is that which appears in the *Tuam News* of 20 Oct. 1899, brought to my attention by Felix Larkin, the leading authority on the history of the *Freeman's Journal*. The grudgingly sparse mention of Byrne in the *Freeman's Journal* of 14 Oct. 1899 fails to mention that Byrne had been an editor of that paper.

2   *FJ*, 30 Dec. 1889.

3. Michael McDonagh, *The Home Rule Movement* (Dublin and London 1920), pp. 207-8. Healy later alleged that two members of the *Freeman's* staff (Byrne and E.H. Ennis) were sent to London to intimidate the Irish Party, and that one of them, in preferring Parnell to Home Rule, had declared 'To Hell with Home Rule!' Byrne's angry denial was pointedly limited to the allegation only insofar as it related to himself, *National Press*, 27 Aug. 1891, *FJ*, 28 Aug. 1891.

4. F.S.L. Lyons, *Charles Stewart Parnell* (London 1977, repr. 1978), hereinafter cited as Lyons, *Parnell*, pp. 540-1.

5. *FJ*, 8 Dec. 1890, 28 Aug. 1891, 30 Dec. 1889.

6. *Ibid.*, 28 Aug. 1891.

7. *Ibid.*, 22 Sept. 1891.

8. *Ibid.*, 29 Aug. 1891.

9. *Ibid.*, 29 Aug. 1891.

10. It is possible that Byrne's illness may not tell the whole story, and that he also fell victim of divisions within the Parnellite beleaguered camp in relation to the newspaper's financial difficulties. The correspondence of F.J. Allan, who worked on the paper, with John Redmond reveals a degree of tension, and a readiness on Allan's part to bypass Byrne in dealing with the Parnellite leader; see Redmond Papers, NLI MS. 15, 142, and in particular Allan to Redmond, 27 Oct. 1893, 20 July 1894.

11. Michael McDonagh, *The Home Rule Movement* (Dublin and London 1920), p. 237.

12. T.M. Healy, *Letters and Leaders of My Day* (2 vols, London 1928), ii, p. 385. Healy was pointing to the contrast between Byrne and the trim E.H. Ennis who became Assistant Under-Secretary for Ireland under John Morley.

13. *FJ*, 8 Oct. 1891.

14. A.M. Sullivan, *Old Ireland, Reminiscences of an Irish K.C.* (London 1927), pp. 48-9.

PARNELL: A MEMOIR

1. The Maryborough meeting took place on 26 September 1881. Byrne's paraphrase of Parnell's speech outside the courthouse, and the words quoted, are exactly correct, *FJ*, 27 Sept. 1881.

2. Byrne, as the Special Representative of the *Freeman's Journal*, wrote that at the end of the speech 'he seemed unmoved, but to the careful observer he was deeply touched', *FJ*, 18 Dec. 1889.

3. It is a minor irony that the traveller's employer, Jeremiah James Colman MP, was to be to the fore in the Nonconformist opposition to Parnell after the divorce decree: see John F. Glaser, 'Parnell's Fall and the Nonconformist Conscience', *Irish Historical Studies*, vol. xii, pp. 119-38 (Sept. 1960), at pp. 125-6.

4. The following morning, 20 December 1889, Parnell gave Byrne an interview at Bromborough, Cheshire, before returning to London, which confirmed the general impression of satisfaction with what had transpired at Hawarden. Byrne described the meeting as 'entirely confidential and quite satisfactory'. Nothing had been conclusively settled, pending further consultations between Gladstone and his colleagues. Parnell was 'more than satisfied with the favourable impressions which appear to have been made everywhere'. The Irish leader was 'looking much better than when he started on the short campaign which, if the omens be not deceptive, will have far-reaching results', *FJ*, 21 Dec. 1889.

5. Alfred Robbins observed that while Parnell was an excellent shot with a rifle or revolver – he was not at home with a shotgun – he enjoyed accompanying shooting parties at Aughavanagh rather than joining in the fray, *Birmingham Daily Post*, 14 July 1890.

6. Byrne's piece appeared in the *FJ* on 20 August 1888 as an authoritative declaration ('we have reason to announce . . .') rather than an interview. It stated that the chain of evidence being worked up against the contrivers of the forgeries was already of 'a most extraordinary and perfect character', even though the investigations were only two weeks in progress. Diluting Parnell's dramatic suggestion that J.C. Macdonald, the *Times* manager, would finish in the dock, Byrne wrote that it was believed that John Walter, the editor of the paper, and George Buckle, its proprietor, would profess complete ignorance of the source of the letters brought to them by Macdonald, 'who will refuse to give any evidence before the Commission with the probable result to him of a committal for contempt'.

7. Robbins likewise wrote of Parnell, 'one could not talk to him often without observing that in his cool moments . . . he weighed his words with much deliberation, and obviously chose the precise words he wished remembered', *Parnell, The Last Five Years* (London 1926), p. 27.

8. In fact, Gladstone's successor as the leader of the Liberal Party in 1894 was the Earl of Rosebery, whose enthusiasm for Home Rule scarcely succeeded Harcourt's.

9. Parnell used the quotation in his speech at the National Club, Dublin, on

2 August, regretting William O'Brien's declaration of opposition to his leadership on O'Brien's release from Galway Jail, *FJ*, 3 Aug. 1891. The quotation is from John Greenleaf Whittier:

> For all sad words of tongue or pen,
> The saddest are these: 'it might have been!'

10. For Parnell's peremptory emendation of Thomas Moore's then well-known lines, see also William O'Brien, *The Parnell of Real Life* (London 1926), p. 56.

11. Byrne is observing the exaggerated Victorian convention prohibiting authorial reference to the self.

12. Morley was in Ireland in mid-December 1890 (Morley, *Gladstone* [3 vols, London 1903], p. 452).

13. W.H. Smith, Bookseller, then First Lord of the Treasury and Leader of the House of Commons.

14. John Walter, proprietor of *The Times*.

15. Henry Labouchere (1831-1912), pro-Home Rule Radical member of parliament for Northampton, newspaperman, cynic, and wit. Labouchere was celebrated for the observation that while he did not object to Gladstone always having the ace of trumps up his sleeve, he took exception to his insistence that God had put it there.

16. Hartington, later the Duke of Devonshire, led the 'Whigs' who split with the Gladstonian Liberals on Home Rule, along with the radical opponents of Home Rule led by Chamberlain.

17. Archbishop Croke of Cashel

18. L.H. Courtney, Liberal Unionist MP.

19. Philip Callan, a recalcitrant Nationalist MP, was ousted from the representation of North Louth in December 1885 after a vigorous campaign against him by Parnell.

20. The nationalist weekly, *United Ireland*, was established by Parnell in February 1881. Its editorial policy, determined by William O'Brien, with vigorous assistance from T.M. Healy until the Galway election of February 1886, was, in nationalist terms, well to the left of Parnell's. The paper's attacks on Spencer, Trevelyan and Balfour were, as the phrases cited by Byrne reveal, notably virulent.

21. Lord Spencer, Lord Lieutenant of Ireland, 1868-74 and 1882-5.

22. George Otto Trevelyan, Chief Secretary for Ireland, May 1882-Oct. 1884.

23. Abbreviation of the 'Grand Old Man', Gladstone's political soubriquet.

24. Lord Aberdeen was the lord-lieutenant in Gladstone's first Home Rule administration of 1886.

25. The construction in the Plan of Campaign of the 'town' of 'New Tipperary', an early revelation of nationalist deficiencies in the matter of town planning, proved a financial, legal and political disaster.

26. Patrick Egan (1841-1919), a Dublin Fenian, was a founder member and treasurer of the Irish National Land League, who remained an influential political activist after his emigration to the United States.

27. The Special Commission, known variously as the 'Parnell Commission', or 'the *Times* Commission', sat between 17 September 1888 and 22 No-

vember 1889, charged with conducting an enquiry into the *Times* allegations against Parnell and others, arising out of, though not confined to, the Pigott forgeries.

28. Parnell's controversial speech at Cincinnati was delivered on 23 February 1880; see generally Lyons, *Parnell* (London 1977, repr. 1978), pp. 110-3.

29. *The Irish World,* the flamboyantly extreme Irish-American paper of Patrick Ford (1837-1914), who emigrated with his parents from Galway to the United States at the age of four, achieved notoriety for its invitation to readers to subscribe to its 'skirmishing fund'.

30. Anna Parnell (1852-1911).

31. Sir Henry Drummond Wolff, Conservative MP, and 'Fourth Party' ally of Randolph Churchill.

32. Edmund Dwyer Gray *père*, proprietor of the *Freeman's Journal*, and influential Nationalist MP.

33. Parnell's meeting with Carnarvon took place on 1 August 1885. Early the previous month Carnarvon had met Justin McCarthy; see Lyons, *Parnell*, pp. 283-7.

34. *United Ireland*, 18 Aug. 1888.

35. The clash between Parnell and Chamberlain arose in the course of the debates on the Special Commission in August 1888; see Lyons, *Parnell*, pp. 395-402.

POSTSCRIPT: PARNELL AND THE PRESS

1. *New York Times*, 7 Aug. 1887; see also T.P. O'Connor, 'The Rule of the Purse', *Contemporary Review*, vol. 37, pp. 990-1103. The late Stephen Koss has written of the 'phalanx of Irish scribes' in the 1880 parliament (Stephen Koss, *The Rise and Fall of the Political Press in Britain* [London 1981, repr. 1990], p. 216). In the pre-nationalist era, such was the predominance of Irishmen among the reporters in the House of Commons that William Cobbett referred to them derisively as 'rayporthers', Michael McDonagh, *Parliament* (Westminster 1902), pp. 337-8.

2. T.M. Healy, 'A Great Man's Fancies', *Westminster Gazette*, 2 Nov. 1893; *Pall Mall Gazette*, interview, 8 Dec. 1890.

3. Koss, *op. cit.*, p. 238; Michael McDonagh, *The Reporter's Gallery* (London 1913), pp. 56 *et seq.*

4. Robbins, *Parnell, The Last Five Years*, p. 33.

5. Ibid., pp. 27, 38.

6. Ibid., p. 181; my italics.

7. Ibid., p. 33.

8. *FJ*, 9 Oct. 1891; *Pall Mall Gazette*, 8 Oct. 1891.

9. *United Ireland*, 8 Oct. 1891, 'An Irish Reporter's Tribute'; see also *United Ireland*, 5 Oct. 1895, 'A Reporter's Tribute', by 'C'.

10. *Irish Packet*, 26 Mar. 1904; *FJ*, 26 Dec. 1890.

11. R.B. O'Brien, *The Life of Charles Stewart Parnell* (2 vols, London 1898), ii, pp. 350-1.

CHRONOLOGY

1846	27 June	Birth of Parnell, at Avondale, Co. Wicklow
1874	18 March	Parnell loses his first by-election, for County Dublin
1875	17 April	Parnell elected for Meath
1880	April	General election; Parnell returned for Meath and Cork, and elects to sit for Cork
	17 May	Parnell elected leader of the Irish Party, 23-18
		Parnell meets Katharine O'Shea
1880-1	28 Dec.-23 Jan.	State prosecution of Parnell and others
1881-2	13 Oct.-2 May	Parnell imprisoned in Kilmainham Jail
	6 May	Murder of Lord Frederick Cavendish, Chief Secretary, and T. H. Burke, his Under-Secretary, in the Phoenix Park, Dublin
1885	Nov.-Dec.	General election leaves Parnell with the balance of power
1886	30 Jan.	Gladstone invited to form a government
	10 Feb.	Galway by-election: Captain W. H. O'Shea returned, after Parnell's intervention
	8 April	Gladstone introduces Home Rule Bill
	8 June	Defeat of Home Rule Bill
	July	General election returns unionist majority
1888	17 Sept.-22 Nov. 89	Hearings of the Special Commission to inquire into the Times' 'Parnellism and Crime' allegations

1889	29 Feb.	Suicide of Richard Pigott
	18-19 Dec.	Parnell meets Gladstone at Hawarden
	24 Dec.	Captain W. H. O'Shea files divorce petition against his wife, Katharine, naming Parnell as co-respondent
1890	13 Feb.	Report of the Special Commission
	15, 17 Nov.	Hearing of divorce petition; Captain granted divorce decree nisi
	20 Nov.	T. M. Healy, Justin McCarthy and others endorse Parnell's leadership at the Leinster Hall, Dublin
	25 Nov.	Irish Party re-elects Parnell as its sessional chairman; Gladstone publishes letter to Morley declaring that Parnell's continued leadership of the Irish Party would render his own leadership of the Liberal Party 'almost a nullity'
	29 Nov.	Publication of Parnell's 'Manifesto to the Irish People'
	1-6 Dec.	Irish Party meets to consider Parnell's leadership and splits 45-28 against Parnell
	21 Dec.	First by-election of the split, North Kilkenny:

First by-election of the split, North Kilkenny:

Sir John Pope-Hennessy (Anti-Parnellite)	2527
Vincent Scully (Parnellite)	1362
Anti-Parnellite majority	1165

| 1891 | 30 Dec.- 11 Feb. | Abortive negotiations at Boulogne between William O'Brien, John Dillon and Parnell |
| | 1 April | Second by-election of the split, North Sligo: |

Second by-election of the split, North Sligo:

Bernard Collery (Anti-Parnellite)	3261
V. B. Dillon (Parnellite)	2493

	Anti-Parnellite majority	768

25 June	Parnell marries Katharine O'Shea

27 June	Parnell's forty-fifth birthday

6 July — Third by-election of the split, Carlow

John Hammond (Anti-Parnellite)	3755
A. J. Kettle (Parnellite)	1539
Anti-Parnellite majority	2216

30 July — John Dillon and William O'Brien declare against Parnell on their release from Galway Jail

24 Sept. — The *Freeman's Journal* changes course and declares against Parnell

27 Sept. — Parnell addresses his last meeting, at Creggs

6 Oct. — Death of Parnell at Brighton

BIBLIOGRAPHICAL NOTE

'Mr Parnell's figure', *The Spectator* lamented shortly after his election as leader of the Irish Party in 1880, 'is but too likely to become historical.' The myth of the Irish leader began to accrete remarkably early. Throughout his career, Parnell attracted close and fascinated press attention, in which biography was implicit. *A Life of Charles Stewart Parnell, with an Account of his Ancestry*, by the Irish journalist Thomas Sherlock, appeared as early as 1881. T.P. O'Connor's *The Parnell Movement* followed in 1886. Within days of Parnell's death, O'Connor published his *Charles Stewart Parnell, A Memory*. Before the year was out *The Uncrowned King: The Life and Public Services of Charles Stewart Parnell*, by Robert M. McWade, was published in Philadelphia.

The ensuing decade was a requiem for the Irish leader. Within the commemorative cult there was a conscious endeavour to salvage and preserve memories of Parnell by those who had known him. Reminiscences of Parnell appeared on the anniversaries of his death in the Parnellite papers, the *Irish Weekly Independent* and *United Ireland*. Of these, Edward Byrne's memoir is the most extended and biographically important.

It is significant that the published works which most vividly convey the spirit of Parnellism after Parnell were written by women. Jenny Wyse-Power published in 1892 her excellent compilation, *Words of the Dead Chief, Being Extracts from the Public Speeches and Other Pronouncements of Charles Stewart Parnell, from the Beginning to the Close of his Memorable Life*. In her introduction, Anna Parnell, faithful to her severe insistence on the impersonality of political principles, made no reference whatever to family connections. Katharine Tynan's several memoirs vividly convey the embattled exhilaration of Parnellite allegiance: *Twenty Five Years: Reminiscences* (1913); *The Middle Years* (1916); *Memories* (1924). Margaret Leamy's *Parnell's Faithful Few*, published in New York in 1936, limns the personalities who made up the post-split Parnellite party.

The appearance in 1898 of *The Life of Charles Stewart Parnell* by Richard Barry O'Brien, the London Irish journalist, writer, and friend of Parnell, marked the acme of the Parnellite commemorative enterprise. One of the great nineteenth-century biographies, part memoir, part history, it remains an indispensable source. Its publication moreover elicited three important responses: W.E.H. Lecky's two-part review (in *The Spectator*, 19, 26 November 1898), which stands as a coda to his *Leaders of Public Opinion in Ireland* of 1871; J.L. Garvin's

Carlylean 'Parnell and his Power' (*Fortnightly Review*, 1 December 1898); and Lionel Johnson's 'The Man who would be King' (*The Academy*, 19 November 1889). Further reminiscences came much later, notably John Howard Parnell's *Charles Stewart Parnell, A Memoir* (1916), and Sir Alfred Robbins' *Parnell, the Last Five Years* (1926).

The most personal testament to Parnell is Katharine Parnell's *Charles Stewart Parnell; His Love Story and Political Life* (1914). While written in the shadow of her son, Gerard, who evidently shared many of his father's less engaging characteristics, her book conveys the fiercely exigent mutual preoccupation that characterized her relations with Parnell – is convincing, and even compelling. Henry Harrison's *Parnell Vindicated* (1931), which records the account Katharine gave him shortly after Parnell's death, and his more tendentious *Parnell, Joseph Chamberlain and Mr Garvin* (1938), movingly exemplify the decency of allegiance of Parnell's parliamentary loyalists.

The spectre of Parnell stalks the memoirs of the split's combatants. Michael Davitt's sour, even obtuse, but important, *Fall of Feudalism in Ireland*, was published in 1904. William O'Brien's *Parnell of Real Life* (1926) is derivative of his three earlier volumes of memoirs, *Recollections* (1905), *An Olive Branch in Ireland* (1910), and *Evening Memories* (1920). His writings reflect the eccentrically shifting alignments of his later career, and, split-tormented elegies for Parnell, they strikingly convey the lost direction of Irish politics in the post-Parnell era.

Of the memoirs written by the survivors of the split, T. M. Healy's *Letters and Leaders of my Day* (1928) is the most psychologically arresting. Highly precocious and compulsively ambitious, Healy was compelled to witness at close quarters what he had long apprehended, Parnell's rise to greatness: Parnell in turn intuited Healy's inchoate disloyalty, before its consummation, and excluded him from his confidence. Healy's letters, candidly venomous even in their edited form, reveal the remarkably early germination of his resentment of Parnell. By contrast, T.P. O'Connor's *Memoirs of an Old Parliamentarian* (1929) are disappointingly bland, a compilation of anecdotes and characterizations dulled and worn by a lifetime's repetition.

Conor Cruise O'Brien's classic *Parnell and his Party* (1957), the first modern scholarly treatment of Parnell and Parnellism, still defines the state of the art. F.S.L. Lyons, whose *Irish Parliamentary Party 1890-1910* surveyed the political aftermath of Parnell, chronicled the split in *The Fall of Parnell* (1958). His biography of John Dillon (1968) extended over the long span of the Irish Party's existence. His *Charles Stewart Parnell* (1977) is the consolidating modern biography, and likely to remain so. T.W. Moody's *Davitt and the Irish Revolution 1846-82* (1981) provides a magisterial survey of the agrarian and Fenian context of Parnell's early career. R.F. Foster's elegiac *Charles Stewart Parnell: A Man and his Family* (1977) renders the lost dynasty against the setting of Avondale, and of the Anglo-Irish patriot tradition. Paul Bew's *C.S. Parnell* (1980) is a short, intelligent left-wing assessment of Parnell's career.